Lady of Parham

By David Edgecombe

Caribbean
Reads

Second Edition

ISBN: 978-0-9908659-4-0

Library of Congress Control Number: 2014952393

Text copyright © 2014 David Edgecombe

Published by CaribbeanReads Publishing,

Basseterre, St. Kitts.

All rights reserved.

Printed in the USA

For Pam and Percy Arthurton

Table of Contents

Preface

I was handed the story of *Lady of Parham* in November 2012 at dinner in Antigua with my dear friends Pam and Percy Arthurton. Pam was intrigued by a local legend of a ghost who haunts the village of Parham and cannot go to her final resting place until she tells someone where she hid the treasure she stole and buried four centuries ago.

Pam had done considerable research on the legend, using resources from the Museum of Antigua and Barbuda and the Historic Society. I pored over the four typewritten pages of notes she gave me that consisted mainly of eye-witness reports from persons who over the centuries claimed to have encountered the ghost. While these were interesting, I was more intrigued by the human elements of the story: man's ceaseless fascination with easy treasure, the greed for gold which influences behavior even after death, and the ghosts that haunt every generation.

The other compelling reason for writing the play was Pam's interest in it as a commercial venture. I have implicit confidence in her business acumen and know how badly Caribbean theatre suffers from not having the sustained interest of good entrepreneurs. She thought a play about the legend of Parham could make great dinner theatre. I thought a musical would make the best dinner theatre. However, since I know little about dinner theatre or musicals—although I've toyed with writing a musical for years—I decided to work in the medium I know best and set out to write a play. Musicals and dinners would follow.

At the time Pam introduced the legend to me, I was still working on cleaning up my stage adaptation of the short story *Kill the Rabbits* by Tiffany Yanique that premiered at the University of the Virgin Islands in Spring 2012, and producing the movie Timeless, written and directed by Edward LaBorde, Jr., that, at the time of writing, is still in production. I couldn't focus on *Lady of Parham*, but she stayed on my back burner and little by little ideas germinated around the story and how to tell it. These ideas became more refined following my August 2013 visit to the village of Parham in Antigua.

I went to the house where Sarah Rumsey and her husband Patrick lived in the late 17th Century before Sarah became *the ghost*. It was in that house that she murdered Thomas Flynn, her husband's uncle, for the oak chest of gold and silver he brought with him from Ireland. It is said she buried the treasure at or in the surroundings of a lodge about 300 yards from the house, but there was no trace of this lodge. The current occupant of the Rumsey plantation house knew of the ghost, but had never seen her. He told me that he hoped she would visit him soon and point him to some of the gold as he happened to be a bit 'broke' at that time.

I came across an old school building that had been transformed into a community center. It would later influence the setting of the play. I met many people in Antigua and the Virgin Islands who were familiar with the story. The younger ones say they vaguely remember hearing about it from their parents and grand parents. One told me Parham is the obeah capital of Antigua although others argue the title more accurately belongs to Potters. I found the folklore of

Parham fascinating and left convinced that it was a great setting for a ghost story.

From my research, I learned there are at least two other plays in existence about the ghost of Parham. One I could find no information on. The other is by the playwright Oliver Flax, who I never met but whose name I remember well as the author of The *Legend of Prince Klaas*, the play Antigua took to the first ever CARIFESTA in Guyana in 1972. I learned with regret of his passing in 2013 in Trinidad where he had lived for several years. I have not yet been able to secure any copies of his plays.

I knew from the beginning I couldn't just write another ghost story—whatever that is. I wanted to dramatize the interplay between the past and present, juxtaposing the problems and challenges of modern day persons against those of people in the past, all in the context of the Parham legend. The cast had to be small, so each actor would need to play multiple characters. It was also important that the production adapt a minimalist style. A simple set with simple props and simple costume changes was all the actors would get to move from the 21st to the 17th century and back. A change of accent and attitude would convert a black Antiguan into a white European. A brief walk across the stage would take the audience 400 years into the past. It would be an actors' piece that would take full advantage of theatre's greatest attribute—the willingness of its audience to suspend disbelief.

A year passed. I had some ideas and had made a few notes but not one line of the play had been written. On December 20 I found myself stuck at the Frenchtown Deli, St. Thomas. The niece of a friend came into the deli and we struck up a conversation in which I told her about the play. Moments after she left her aunt strolled in and wanted to hear about the play as well. In telling them, most of the remaining knotty problems with characters and plot straightened themselves out to the point where I knew it was time to begin writing.

I called a friend and asked if she could record me telling her the play. She agreed and sent me a transcript of the recording so quickly it was dazzling. I began writing early the morning of December 21 and typed "The End" on January 2, 2014. I always try to write my first drafts quickly but this was the fastest I had ever done one. Then came the long process of rewriting and editing that continued through rehearsal to the world premier at the UVI Little Theatre on April 4, to the first staging of the full play in August and to its performance at the 6th Nature Island Literary Festival (NILF) in Dominica on August 9th.

The play calls for just five actors: Tulip, Justin, Sauna, Kyle, and Mabel, but, casting proved a monumental task.

Tulip is a central member of the group that meets at the old school house. I chose the name Tulip because all the Tulips I know are from Antigua and I liked using a name I thought of as typically Antiguan. Tulip also plays Sarah, the Lady of Parham.

Justin, her live-in boyfriend, also plays Patrick, Sarah's husband. In a way Justin is Patrick's second chance to get things right, to get and keep a good woman who can possibly save him from his greatest fear—becoming a 'nobody'.

Sauna, Tulip's niece, also plays the slave girl Sofia and the mysterious woman in Paris who descends from the ghost.

Kyle, her boyfriend, also plays Uncle Tom, the slave boy Clem and Jack Collins.

Mabel, the last member of the group, doubles as the narrator. The entire ghost story is in her head and she's the energy of the play. In effect, as Mabel goes, so goes the play. I didn't see this until deep into rehearsals.

The first actor chosen to play Mabel was Manefa O'Connor, a senior at the University of the Virgin Islands who was due to graduate just a few weeks after the show opened. The demands of school conflicted with the demands of the production and it became obvious that she was struggling. Her primary obligation was to graduate and so I replaced her less than a week before we opened.

Her replacement was Heather Hogarth-Smith, UVI's registrar at the time, who had given an excellent portrayal of Miss Aggie in Trevor Rhone's Old Story Time that I had directed two years before. Heather was already part of the production, working with Manefa on her lines, so she was familiar with the part. She agreed to try to learn the role in the little time we had and we set out to make it happen. But I had made a mistake; it was simply not enough time. The final dress rehearsal was a mess and I pulled no punches in letting the company know this.

At 11:40 that night I got a text from Heather, withdrawing from the play. I panicked and fired off a response asking her to sleep on it before making that decision. As soon as I pushed 'Send' I saw with blinding clarity that she was right. Nothing could be done to prepare her to open in just a few hours. I fired off another text telling her on reflection she had made the right call. It was up to me to deal with it.

My mind flashed back to an incident in high school that was one of the most valuable lessons I ever learned. I have written about this before.

While I was president of the Montserrat Secondary School Dramatic Society we took a play to a University of the West Indies Theatre workshop in Antigua in 1968. Minutes before we were to perform there was an electricity blackout.

A tall elegant woman whose name I don't recall said, "Get the actors ready, you're going on."

"Without lights?" I asked.

She said, "Just get yourselves ready now."

I was adamant. "We're not going on without lights."

"And what should we say to the hundreds of people sitting out there in the audience?"

There was indeed a large gathering in the open-air auditorium with only the light of the moon to see by. I shrugged. That wasn't my problem.

"Listen young man," she said, "The one immutable law of theatre is, the show must go on. We will use flambeaux, or searchlights, or catch fireflies and put them in a bottle, if we have to, but the show must go on."

And so it did. Shortly before the play ended the electric lights came back on and ruined the warm, cozy embrace we had developed with the audience in the soft flambeaux lighting.

Lady of Parham was going on as scheduled.

I sent the following email to the company:

It is at times like this, when your back is against the wall, that theatre really gets exciting. Heather did an honorable thing last night. Instead of simply not showing up tonight, she gave me as much notice as she could that she has quit the show. Here is her text:

"David, so many things didn't work tonight, there is no way a few hours tomorrow can be a fix. In addition to not being well I am dealing with a personal matter that has a deadline tomorrow. I have taken the somewhat difficult decision to call it a day with the play and wish to give you the extra hours overnight to do what needs to be done. I feel badly tonight and don't expect to feel any better tomorrow night."

I understand and respect Heather's decision. Her health and wellbeing should be first. I want her to be well. And I appreciate her giving me as much notice as she could.

You feel devastated? Disappointed? Crushed? Don't be! The show must go on. That is the most immutable law of theatre: THE SHOW MUST GO ON! So we'll have a show tonight. Let's make it the best show there ever was.

I went on stage that night (and for the next seven performances) with script in hand and read the role of Mabel at the UVI Little Theatre, St. Thomas. Many audience members said that all I needed was a dress and wig to ace the part. My response? "Tyler Perry already has the patent on that and I can't risk an infringement."

About a month after that first run, UVI Theatre was invited to stage Lady of Parham at the NILF in Dominica. I welcomed this as an opportunity to see the play staged with a full cast for the first time. We had to rehearse with a new Mabel, stage three performances in St. Thomas then head to Dominica.

I wish it could be that easy, but experience should have taught me otherwise. The actors playing Tulip and Sauna were not available to tour, and of course, we had no Mabel. The only two actors from the original cast were Jerome Kendall and his son Jelani who played Justin and Kyle respectively. We assembled a cast and started to rehearse again.

One night at rehearsal I got an email from our new Tulip announcing her withdrawal from the play. Jerome Kendall, a comrade in arms in over 20 years of productions and Afreekan Southwell, the stage manager and a pillar of support over many years of productions, sat at a bar sadly weighing our options when the new Sauna called to tell me she was quitting as well. In my long theatre journey, strewn with obstacles and setbacks, I had never once felt genuinely defeated until that night.

Afreekan said, "Don't give up. Go home and sleep on it. But don't give up."

I went to sleep wondering if the Lady was haunting my play and if I should head post haste to Parham or Potters for a bath.

The next day the new Sauna changed her mind about dropping out of the play. The hill that had turned into Mount Kilimanjaro the night before was once again just another ordinary steep hill. With less than two weeks to opening, we were still without a Tulip/Sarah. I called in a favor from a wonderful actor I had worked with in St. Croix two years ago. She was now studying in New York for her Masters in Fine Arts (Acting). She arrived three days later ready to get to work but with an expired passport she had left in NY.

We went to work on fixing the passport issue as we jumped into an intense rehearsal schedule with Jerome Kendal as Justin and Jelani Kendall as Kyle. They were joined by Marie Paul as Mabel, Junia Washington as Sauna, and Oceana James as Tulip. We had ten days to rehearse before performing the play with a full cast for the first time in St. Thomas, then one week later in Dominica. I'm pleased to say *Lady of Parham* was joyfully received on both islands.

Dominica turned out to be particularly special. To mark the 450th Anniversary of William Shakespeare's birth year, the Nature Island Literary Festival featured drama. As a result I got to see thee plays staged by three of my dear theatre buddies Alwin Bully, Dorbrene O'Marde, and Felix Fleming.

Alwin revised his play, *The Ruler*, that was a huge hit when first produced in 1977. I was pleased to see it for the first time. Dorbrene revived his delightful play, *This World Spin One Way*, which had its world premiere at the Reichhold Center for the Arts, University of the Virgin Islands in 1997, directed by Jean Small. And Felix Fleming gave a wonderful presentation of Athold Fugard's well-known play, *Sizwi Banzi is Dead*. The four of us share a common journey of writing, directing and producing plays for well over 40 years in a close to barren theatre landscape.

I'm pleased with the response that *Lady of Parham* has drawn and the interest many have expressed in seeing it performed. I hope that Pam Atherton gets her wish for this play's commercial success. I wish that you enjoy reading this script and that you have the opportunity to enjoy a performance of the play soon.

David

23 October, 2014

Acknowledgements

For reading the first draft and providing beneficial insight, thanks to Erika Waters, Carol Mitchell, and Ashley Bernier.

For proofreading, thanks to Sharlene Harris.

For going beyond his role as actor by supporting and sharing his insight with the rest of the cast and for his ideas for the set, thanks to Jerome Kendall.

And for his support on every front and in every aspect of the production, thank you to Afreekan Southwell.

Productions

Lady of Parham was first staged at the Little Theatre at the University of the Virgin Islands on April 4th, 2014. It was directed by the author.

Cast in Order of Appearance

KYLE/Uncle/Jack Collins	Jelani Kendall
SAUNA/Sofie/Paris Lady	Akela Brumant
JUSTIN/Patrick	Jerome Kendall
MABEL	David Edgecombe*
TULIP/Sarah	Chanice Williams

*On the night before the play opened, the actor playing Mabel withdrew from the play. Evoking the time-honored theatre tradition that "the show must go on", the author/director read the role of Mabel for the first eight performances of the play.

The play was remounted in St. Thomas August 1-4, 2014 in preparation for a staging at the Nature Island Literary Festival in Dominica on August 9.

Cast in Order of Appearance

SAUNA/Sofie/Paris Lady	Junia Washington
KYLE/Uncle/Jack Collins	Jelani Kendall
JUSTIN/Patrick	Jerome Kendall
MABEL	Marie Paul
TULIP/Sarah	Oceana James

xii

Production Unit

Director:	David Edgecombe
Tech. Director/Lighting:	Doug Salisbury
Stage Manager/Drummer:	Afreekan Southwell
Lighting Design:	Corrine Linquist Daniel & Doug Salisbury
Sound Design:	Stefan Todman & Joe Barzey
Wardrobe Design/Creation:	Dena Fisher & Jahweh David
Set Design:	Jerome Kendal, Dena Fisher, & Afreekan Southwell
Choreographer:	Marie Paul
Dance Consultant:	Monty Thompson
Sound Operator:	Joe Barzey
Master Builders:	Dr. Douglas Larch & Afreekan Southwell
Assisted by:	Deeno Cumberbatch & Julie Cruz
Graphics & Poster:	Louis Ibel, Jr.
Assistant to the Director:	Shanice Laurent

Characters

SAUNA/Sofie/Paris Lady A young woman, 20.
KYLE/Uncle/Jack Collins A university student, 23.
JUSTIN/Patrick A building contractor, costume designer and maker, 45.
MABEL A retired drama teacher, 58 and Narrator.
TULIP/Sarah A LIAT flight attendant, 36.

Setting

The set is an old discarded school hall. There is an open stage with a step in front that runs the length of the stage. There are step-ups onto the stage from Right and Left and Up Centre as well. There are many scene changes but almost no physical set changes. The actors define the setting, which can change quickly, by how they use the space and what they say. They are aided greatly by lighting, minimum costuming, and a carefully produced soundscape.

As the play opens actors come into the old building that was once an elementary school and is now used as a community centre for various activities including serving as a mass camp.

Time

The action occurs in the present, but goes all the way back to 1656, 1866 and other periods in between.

Lady of Parham

By David Edgecombe

Act I

(In the darkness, Sauna and Kyle enter laughing joyfully)

SAUNA

You are too funny.

KYLE

You could see?

SAUNA

No.

KYLE

Ah mean enough to get the lights while I fasten back the door?

SAUNA

Wha' we need lights for?

KYLE

I'll do it.

SAUNA

Seriously, Kyle, wha' you turning on the lights for?

(Kyle turns on the lights)

KYLE

Ah fraid de dark.

SAUNA

Fraid you shadow is more like it.

KYLE

Fraid *you* is more like it.

1

SAUNA

Oh, you fraid me now? Is about time.

(She tries to kiss him)

KYLE

Cool out, nuh man. Where everybody?

SAUNA

Why you fraid me, Kyle?

KYLE

Not a soul here but us.

SAUNA

An' wha' we doing about it?

(Pause. He looks directly at her)

What you doing about it, mister?

(He walks slowly towards her. She embraces him passionately and they kiss. He wants to break off, she won't let him. He unhooks her arms from around his neck and walks away. She runs in front of him and they stand looking at each other in silence. She takes his right hand and plants it on her right breast. Then she plants his left hand on her left breast and holds them in place)

KYLE

Not here, Sauna. Not like this.

SAUNA

Tell me they doan feel good.

KYLE

This is not the place or time, you know that.

SAUNA

I know with my foolish parents, we don't have the luxury of either right space or right time. We have to work with what we have.

KYLE

I will talk with them.

SAUNA

You crazy?

KYLE

I'll go talk to your father.

SAUNA

You have a death wish?

KYLE

He goin' kill me?

SAUNA

Yes, he will kill you.

KYLE

Then I'll talk to you mother.

SAUNA

Well, she wouldn't kill you, but sooner or later he will hear.

KYLE

Exactly. So what I'm saying is let's make it sooner rather than later.

SAUNA

Let's? Me ain' in that with you, brother. You on you own with that.

KYLE

Let me ask you something, Sauna, why you fraid you father so?

SAUNA

You don't know the man, Kyle. If you did you wouldn't ask.

KYLE

I'm asking to get to know him.

SAUNA

No...no. It's...it's not that easy.

KYLE

Okay. One Sunday afternoon, let's say, I pull up at your house...

SAUNA

What house?

KYLE

You father house.

SAUNA

You and wha' army of thugs?

KYLE

So I go to his office then. Make an appointment.

SAUNA

And how exactly is that done?

KYLE

I say to his personal assistant, I need to speak with Mr. Athill immediately. It's important.

SAUNA

Do you have an appointment?

KYLE

No, but…

SAUNA

Mr. Athill sees no one without an appointment. You can't just walk off the street demanding to see Mr. Athill, that's not how it works.

KYLE

Tell him Sauna's boyfriend wants to talk to him.

SAUNA

What!!?

KYLE

Yes, tell him his daughter's man out here to see him.

SAUNA

And what should I tell him you wish to speak to him about?

KYLE

A personal matter.

SAUNA

Is breed you come here to tell Mr. Athill you breed off he daughter? De apple o' he eye? De man one an' only daughter?

KYLE

No, not that. Tell him Sauna and I seeing each other secretly for two months now. Sneaking and hiding like two ole rat tiefing corn and ah done with that shit now.

SAUNA

Done with it?

KYLE

Yes. Done with it. I want to come to the house to see her, pick her up from there. Sit in the living room and wait for her if she's not ready. Bring her home when we're done. And if it's early enough, sip cocktails with her on the verandah enjoying the view. And, I wouldn't object if every now and then I'm invited to have Sunday lunch with the family.

(A long pause. She leads him to a seat)

SAUNA

Let me explain this to you, Kyle. Maybe, just maybe, after you come back as an engineer, and you have a job, and a house, and a car, and a plane, and a yacht my father might listen to that from you.

KYLE

And you?

SAUNA

What you mean and you?

KYLE

This is how you want us to operate? In darkness and secrecy?

(Justin enters and looks around)

JUSTIN

Only you two lovebirds reach? Where the others?

KYLE

Lovebirds?

JUSTIN

Yes, mister man, lovebirds.

KYLE

Why you say that?

SAUNA

Nobody else come yet.

JUSTIN

You think the little pantomime the two of you playing
out have anybody fool?

SAUNA

Nobody else come yet.

JUSTIN

Ah see that. Just look at the two of you. Thinking the
rest of us born big so.

KYLE

That's what we here to deal with tonight?

JUSTIN

De only thing ah doan know is if you get any yet. An'
that's because you so damn slow.

SAUNA

Oh puuleeeze!

JUSTIN

Hey you, you li ghel, you still have you maid?

SAUNA

How is that you frigging business, Justin?

KYLE

Justin! You gone too far now, man.

7

JUSTIN

All right! All right! Just wanted to mess with you heads little bit.

SAUNA

God damn it!

JUSTIN

I apologize.

SAUNA

God damn you to hell.

JUSTIN

I said I apologize. What the hell is wrong with you?

SAUNA

No! What the hell is wrong with you? No wonder nobody coming to join you stupid carnival troupe.

JUSTIN

Hey, don't go there.

SAUNA

This is our third meeting, where the 30, 50, 100 members we suppose to have?

JUSTIN

Kyle, please ask this…bi…woman, not to go there.

SAUNA

Go ahead, man, don't stop. Lay de B word on me. Hit me wid it.

JUSTIN

I moved away from it. Ah carefully an' deliberately didn go there.

SAUNA

You think because you give Kyle a little holiday job you have the right to abuse him? This is a man who goin' be an engineer, with a degree. A sober one, not like...

KYLE

Cool out, Sauna, would you please just calm down?

SAUNA

You siding with him?

KYLE

No. Is not that. Justin didn't just give me a holiday job. Whatever and wherever I am today is because of him.

SAUNA

Well, it certainly doesn't give him the right to abuse me.

KYLE

Abuse? What abuse?

JUSTIN

No, she asking an important question. Where all the people in truth?

SAUNA

Exactly.

JUSTIN

How many you invite?

SAUNA

None.

JUSTIN

You Kyle?

KYLE

15…20. Many say they not leaving their troupe…

JUSTIN

See? Stuck in de same ole same ole, battening down in their burrows.

KYLE

Some say dey done with carnival, except for wine, woman and song.

JUSTIN

Dropouts! Setting the example. Feeding the dropout epidemic in our schools, in our society.

KYLE

A handful did say they would come.

JUSTIN

You see them? Whey dey be? Where are they?

(Mabel enters)

MABEL

I'm right here.

JUSTIN

You late.

MABEL

Sorry. Five people promised to come with me. I waited, I waited, and I waited. In the end, all five had some lousy excuse why they couldn't come.

JUSTIN

Where Tulip?

MABEL

She not here?

JUSTIN

You see her?

MABEL

Hey, I aint putting up with any of you nonsense to-night you know, Justin.

SAUNA

What ah tell you? What a tell you, Kyle?

JUSTIN

Look, ah done. Go long bout all you business. All o' you. Run! Run go team up wid de mediocre posse. And that's the whole of Antigua, de whole frigging Caribbean, if you ask me.

SAUNA

Mr. Nothing but Excellence.

JUSTIN

I am sick and...

MABEL

Stop it! Ah say, stop it right now! That's not the way it's going down either. I don't want to hear any more talk about ah done.

JUSTIN

Okay, with five of us...four of us...what can we do other than be done.

11

MABEL

Here's what I think we should do. I think we should abandon the idea of a troupe.

JUSTIN

But you just said…

MABEL

Yes, I know. We should abandon the idea of a big, new Carnival troupe but not the idea of a first class production.

JUSTIN

About what?

MABEL

About our history. About the way we live. About our folk life and folk tales. Same as you want to do with the troupe.

JUSTIN

With the four of us?

MABEL

Five of us.

JUSTIN

I only see four.

MABEL

You know Tulip is coming.

SAUNA

He well know Auntie Tulip going to be here.

KYLE

Here's what I think, I understand about the history and culture and all that, but why culture always has to mean a coal pot or a hoe or something young people can't relate to?

JUSTIN

So you could learn to relate. Understand you damn roots. Wha' happen to you boy, you doan learn nutn ah teach you?

(He engages Kyle in a mock scuffle pinning him with a chokehold)
Weak lek trush. Stap eat so much damn junk food.

MABEL

Tell him again.

KYLE

All right, all right. Dasheen and tania from now.

SAUNA

Who eating that with you?

KYLE

You. Strictly ital moving forward.

SAUNA

Ah too glad to hear that. Somebody goin' starve for sure, and it ain't me.

KYLE

Ain't me either.

SAUNA

So you goin cook then?

13

SAUNA (Continued)

(Kyle points out to Sauna that they are being watched. She checks herself and addresses Justin and Mabel)

But, joking aside, why we can't portray some de real life drama we living through now?

MABEL
Yes, we must do that too. But since our last meeting Tulip and I been over this and we want to propose that for our first production we enact the Legend of Parham.

SAUNA
What's that?

JUSTIN
She wasn't at our last meeting?

KYLE
She had to leave early, remember?

SAUNA
Ah cyan work with this man, you know. Who could ever work with Justin?

JUSTIN
The more pertinent question is *would* I work with you?

(She is ready to fire back, but Kyle holds her and puts his hand over her mouth)

KYLE
Let this one pass, please.

JUSTIN
And that gets less likely by the minute.

14

MABEL

(Directly to Justin)

You hell bent on messing up, aren't you? Well, don't!

(Pause)

Okay, Sauna, listen up. Legend supported by history has it that around the middle of the 17th Century a young Irish planter by the name of Patrick Rumsey had a thriving plantation here in Parham.

(Tulip enters. Justin who is getting ready to assume the character of Patrick Rumsey sees her)

JUSTIN

Why you so goddamn late?

(She looks at him straight but ignores him otherwise)

TULIP

Anyone heard a strange noise?

(The others laugh)

MABEL

We just getting started.

TULIP

Good. Continue.

JUSTIN

There's no continuing till I get an answer.

TULIP

Tell me again, Justin, what you think gives you the right to talk to me like that?

15

JUSTIN
Try this. You're my woman. You live with me. You...

TULIP
I live with you?

JUSTIN
You are goddam late!

TULIP
I live with you?

JUSTIN
Okay, we live together...

TULIP
We live together, but I'm not your wife. And, sure as hell, I am not your child.

SAUNA
Such a pig! Auntie Tulip, he's a...

TULIP
Shut up, Sauna. Shut up and stay out of this.

JUSTIN
God! Thank you. Thank you.

TULIP
I don't want to hear anything from you either. Let's continue. Where you all reach?

MABEL
I was telling them I think we should go with your idea of presenting the Parham Legend.

16

KYLE

Just the five of us?

MABEL

All of us have creative talent and as we all know, Justin can flip from genius to idiot and back again.

JUSTIN

I'm not so sure about that.

MABEL

We can do it. As a drama teacher for many years I know we can do it.

JUSTIN

All I know is that I'm a mass man. A master at designing and building costumes.

MABEL

And presenting those costumes.

JUSTIN

Clearly not good enough.

TULIP

Because more people didn't come to be in your new troop?

MABEL

You're also a great actor.

JUSTIN

Years since I did any of that.

TULIP

What years? You on stage every day. Come on, Justin, man, let's get on with it. One door close, you open another.

17

JUSTIN

Ah listening.

TULIP

Go on, Mabel.

MABEL

Okay, as I was saying Sauna, young Patrick Rumsey, had a thriving plantation right here in Parham. He also had a young, exceptionally beautiful wife called Sarah,

(Tulip begins her transformation into the character of Sarah)

who was compared by many to such legendary beauties as Cleopatra, Nefertiti, Christina of Sweden...Mabel of Antigua...

(Tulip exits)

Well, sometime in the year of 1656, the young planter got a letter from his Uncle Tom Flynn in Ireland complaining that he was desolate, lonely and in poor health.

(Justin moves into position, donning a shirt that suggests 1656)

This uncle had taught Rumsey all he knew about farming, and had insisted that he learned to read and write. He was the young man's favorite uncle. Patrick was so sorry to hear about his uncle's troubles that he quickly wrote back to him.

(Justin, now in the role of Patrick, sits at his desk in 1656 writing to his uncle in Ireland. He picks up the letter, looks at it and calls out)

PATRICK

Sarah…I say my dear Sarah…

(Tulip enters as Sarah)

SARAH

Now, now, Patrick, why must you make such a terrible din?

PATRICK

I beg your pardon?

SARAH

Why were you shouting so loudly?

PATRICK

Oh? Oh! I wasn't aware…

SARAH

Never mind, dear, what is it you want?

PATRICK

Well, I just responded to my dear Uncle Tom's letter and wondered if you would be so kind to lend a listening ear to what I'm telling him before I send it off to Ireland?

SARAH

Well, yes, of course. I'm frightfully busy so do get on with it.

PATRICK

It should only take a minute.

SARAH

Get on with it.

PATRICK

(Reading)

Dearest Uncle Tom, Words cannot express how greatly it saddened me to learn of your ill health and loneliness in Ireland, but I do think I have the perfect solution: Join me in Antigua and let me and my beautiful wife Sarah look after you.

SARAH

Look after him? My word.

PATRICK

He really is a dear fellow. You'll soon grow to love him as much as I do.

SARAH

I'm just not sure I'm up to looking after anyone.

PATRICK

Wait. Let me go on. I say that, dear uncle, merely as a figure of speech because even if you arrive ill, the beautiful warm climate of Antigua will soon have you on your feet in good health again. You are welcome to farm with me on the modest plantation I'm leasing or to buy land and establish an even grander plantation of your own.

SARAH

He would be in a position to do that?

PATRICK

A hundred times over. If he accepts my offer I think he will sell all of his worldly possessions in Ireland, and arrive here a very, very wealthy man.

SARAH

Hmmmmm.

PATRICK

What?

SARAH

Well, I'm thinking…perhaps…

PATRICK

Out with it.

SARAH

Perhaps we can persuade him to help us buy this modest plantation for ourselves.

PATRICK

I don't want to think of that, Sarah.

SARAH

Why not?

PATRICK

Because I didn't invite him here to help me.

SARAH

Why ever not?

PATRICK

God knows he's done enough of that already. I'm inviting him so I could help him.

SARAH

(She begins to retort but checks herself)
Whatever you say, Patrick, dear. Finish up.

PATRICK

Almost done. Whichever way, I am hoping to see you soon. May the Almighty continue to guide and bless you. Your loving nephew, Patrick.

SARAH

Perfect!

(Sarah exits. Lights fade on the past and come up on Mabel)

MABEL

Uncle Tom loved the idea so much that in six short months he had sold all of his possessions in Ireland and was on his way to Antigua. He arrived with an oaken chest so full of gold and silver, crowns and florins it took six slaves to unload it, get it into a wagon drawn by four mules, up to the plantation house, and eventually into the large room that had been set up as his living quarters.

SAUNA

What kind of money we talking about here?

MABEL

In today money?

SAUNA

Yeah. U.S.

MABEL

Millions!

KYLE

Close to 500 million would be my guess.

SAUNA

For real?

MABEL

Or even more.

SAUNA

Oh-my-god!

KYLE

Continue, please.

MABEL

Well, the Antigua sunshine, and good food were just what uncle needed. He was weak, and pale when he arrived, but in a few days, color returned to his face. Soon he was up and about, regaining his strength and vitality. It was as if God had given him a new lease on life. But, as is always the case, everything did not work out as planned.

(Lights crossfade from present to Sarah and Patrick)

SARAH

When is your uncle finally going to tell us what he intends to do?

PATRICK

In time. I believe he will tell us in due time.

SARAH

In the meantime, he eats our food, he has taken over your favorite horse...

PATRICK

Sarah, he can have all my horses if he wants them. Have a little patience, dear, will you?

23

SARAH

When are you going to ask him for some help so we could buy this plantation?

PATRICK

We are making all of our payments on time, are we not? Not long to go now before we own the land through our own efforts, Sarah. That's what I want us to do.

SARAH

It's been almost a year since he arrived and what has he done?

PATRICK

He was ill.

SARAH

For a minute yes. But with my care, he soon became as healthy as he is today. Now I'm asking you, what is he doing with his good health and, God forbid, all of that money?

PATRICK

Illness is not just about the body. He was wary in spirit. In spirit. You understand that?

SARAH

I understand that you're afraid to tell him he needs to start carrying his own weight.

(Pause)

He is up every morning to catch the sunrise. He was up today even earlier than usual riding off on his horse, your horse. It's almost sunset and where is he?

SARAH (Continued)

He rides all over the island. He goes to the beach. He talks to people everywhere. He has even been seen talking with negroes.

PATRICK

What is wrong with that?

SARAH

In their yards? Sitting down on the floor of their huts?

PATRICK

Really?

SARAH

And get this, eating with them.

PATRICK

No!

SARAH

Well, that one I too refuse to believe.

PATRICK

Shhh! He's coming.

SARAH

He can't be that far gone.

PATRICK

Let me look into it.

(Kyle enters as Uncle)

UNCLE

My dear nephew and beautiful niece, I hope you didn't wait for me to have dinner.

25

PATRICK

You've eaten?

UNCLE

Oh yes.

SARAH

Where?

UNCLE

All over. People all over this island give me food. Perfect strangers invite me to dine with them. And when I leave they give me provisions. I brought back pigeon pea...

SARAH

What's that?

UNCLE

You haven't tried them? Well you should. I'll stew some for you.

SARAH

No thank you!

UNCLE

Ahh, delicious. (Pause.) Perfect strangers bestowing kindness on me. And then...and then...a most remarkable thing happened today.

(Pause)

SARAH

And what might that be?

UNCLE

I saw clearly what I must do with the small fortune God has blessed me with.

SARAH & PATRICK

What?

UNCLE

Give it away.

(Sarah and Patrick gasp)

PATRICK

You're not serious?

UNCLE

I assure you, good nephew, that I am.

PATRICK

Did something bad happen to you today, uncle?

UNCLE

Something remarkable did happen to me.

PATRICK

I mean like sunstroke?

UNCLE

Nothing like that.

PATRICK

Then what?

UNCLE

Why? Because of what I just said?

SARAH

Well…yes! Yes, yes, yes! Do you know how crazy that sounds?

UNCLE

Perhaps to you.

PATRICK

I must confess, Uncle, to me as well, as I'm sure it will to every civilized man on Antigua.

(A long pause)

UNCLE

Today, I had what I believe holy men call an epiphany. On my way back from the beach, I stopped in English Harbor to see this wise old man who over the months has become a dear friend.

SARAH

Who? What is his name?

UNCLE

Old Bob, but the others call him Kintakunte. And so do I.

SARAH

A slave?

UNCLE

Yes.

SARAH

You go all the way to English Habour to visit a slave?

UNCLE

Oh yes.

SARAH

At his hovel?

UNCLE

At his thatch-roofed hut, yes.

SARAH

And you enter into this...hut?

UNCLE

Many times. Sit on the ground with him and the other slaves.

SARAH

Now, please don't tell me you partake of their slop!

UNCLE

They share whatever the have with me. That's why I don't want anything to eat now.

SARAH

Oh, my God, oh my God.

PATRICK

Come my darling, calm yourself.

SARAH

Slop! Pig feet and pig mouth! Chicken foot and giz-zard and neck! Cattle guts and blood. Blood!

UNCLE

And you would be amazed what they do with it.

PATRICK

Amazed?

UNCLE

Oh yes. And something even more amazing hap-pened today.

SARAH

(Getting ready to leave)

I don't want to hear this.

29

UNCLE

No please stay, because it's something I'm hoping you will agree to help me with.

SARAH

I don't think so, Uncle, I don't think so.

PATRICK

Let's hear him out, dear. Please. Go ahead, Uncle.

UNCLE

For weeks now, Kinta has been saying he has something to share with me, but every time I asked him he would say, not yet, as if he needed to test me some more. Today he revealed he has taught himself to read and write English.

PATRICK

No.

UNCLE

Yes, but even more than that he is teaching the children on his plantation to read and write. Even the adults can learn if they want to and some have chosen to.

PATRICK

To what end, Uncle, to what end?

UNCLE

They chose to keep it a secret because they don't know what the planters would say.

SARAH

Surely they could guess.

PATRICK

Surely they are keeping it secret because their instinct tells them it is preposterous and will never be accepted.

UNCLE

He wants me to pave the way so he could teach openly. Black children. And white children too, if they...

PATRICK

(He laughs uproariously)

That's a crazy black fool you're dealing with, Uncle. Surely you see that.

UNCLE

Sitting there in that little hut what I saw were children who under the bleakest of circumstances had learned to read and write and are hungry to learn more. In a bizarre kind of fork lightening flash, I saw what my remaining life's work must be. It was my "Road to Damascus" moment.

SARAH

For God's sake...just tell us.

UNCLE

I knew then I must use my fortune to help Kintakunte accomplish this fabulous goal. First in Ant...

PATRICK

Fabulous goal?

UNCLE

Oh yes. Surely you must see...

31

PATRICK
No, Uncle, no! You have lost your way.

(Uncle laughs)

UNCLE
No, no, my path has never been clearer.

PATRICK
What have these…Africans…done to you?

UNCLE
You regret your education, nephew?

PATRICK
Not at all. But what does that have to do with this?

UNCLE
Was it worth it?

PATRICK
Yes. I would have to say yes.

UNCLE
Think of all the children on this island, black and white, learning how to read and write. And then, all of the children on the other islands as well. It will re-dound to…

SARAH
Utter nonsense. What good will learning to read and write be to a slave?

UNCLE
They will not always be slaves.

SARAH

God intends them to be slaves. He put them on earth to serve us white people as it is said in the Bible.

UNCLE

Where does it say this?

SARAH

Well…everywhere.

UNCLE

Believe me, dear Sarah, slavery is less about black versus white than it is about the powerful preying upon the powerless. You should know that.

SARAH

I've heard enough foolishness from you for a lifetime.

(She turns to walk away)

UNCLE

Wait, Sarah, please…

(She storms off. Patrick tries to restrain her but she brushes him off)

PATRICK

Let her go, Uncle. Let her be.

UNCLE

Did your wife ever tell you her parents were sold into slavery by the British?

PATRICK

Of course not.

UNCLE

It figures.

PATRICK

Why would she tell me that?

UNCLE

Because they were.

PATRICK

Impossible!

UNCLE

I knew them well. Good people, but they fell into debt and the British sold them to a planter in Barbados as slaves.

PATRICK

But she's English.

UNCLE

No. She was raised in England by an aunt, who whisked her out of Ireland before she could be shipped off with her parents. I thought, given this experience, she would be glad to help me deal a blow to slavery.

PATRICK

You are wrong, uncle. I am telling you, you are highly mistaken. Now, if you'll excuse me, I must attend to her.

(Uncle nods as lights cross fade from past to present)

MABEL

One week later uncle was not up before dawn as he usually was for breakfast. He refused lunch, and didn't eat dinner either. Less than a week after, he was dead and buried under a tree in the yard.

SAUNA

Oh my God, oh my God! Dey kill him? She kill him!

MABEL

So it was rumored. The slaves said she mixed iron rust with the seeds of the "Fatiopha" tree growing in the garden, and used it to poison him. But the death certificate from the doctor said he died of yellow fever.

SAUNA

Bet you the doctor was her friend.

MABEL

He was the family doctor.

SAUNA

Told you! I knew it. Had to be.

MABEL

Antigua was having a yellow fever epidemic at the time so it was easy to pass it off as the cause of his death.

(Tulip enters)

TULIP

Sauna, your father here looking for you.

SAUNA

What!

TULIP

Right out there.

SAUNA

Oh Jesus, Jesus!

TULIP
Calm down. Why you panicking?

SAUNA
What you mean why I panicking, Auntie?

TULIP
You didn't tell him you were going out?

SAUNA
Of course.

TULIP
He asked who you in there with and I told him with me working on a production.

SAUNA
That's what I told him.

TULIP
He said somebody came to his office to tell him you have man…

SAUNA
Jesus, god!

TULIP
Sauna, get a hold of yourself! According to him, he's here to take you home, even if he has to come in here and drag you by your hair. Ah said, Vere, go right in there and do that—if you want to lose your daughter for all eternity, and me as well, just so much as set your foot in there.

SAUNA
Let him come.

TULIP

That's more like it. He wants to talk to you.

SAUNA

To say what?

TULIP

Go and see.

SAUNA

Not me! I am doing no such thing.

TULIP

Sauna. Sauna! What have I been telling you?

SAUNA

I know, Auntie, I know...

TULIP

Listen, you're 20 years old, so that makes you a woman. A WOMAN. You hear me? I'm not asking you to disrespect your father. But listen good. Don't let anybody disrespect you either. Not even you poppa. Now go out there and talk to him.

(A long pause)

KYLE

I will come with you.

SAUNA

No, Kyle. I have this.

(Sauna exits)

JUSTIN

Well, we could call it a night.

TULIP

Why?

JUSTIN

That gal ain coming back in here.

TULIP

Bet.

MABEL

You bet, you lose.

JUSTIN

How come she has so much lip for everything else and cyan talk to her father?

MABEL

Look she gone to talk to him now.

TULIP

Exactly.

MABEL

You good, Tulip, I have to hand it to you, you very good.

TULIP

Practice.

MABEL

Nah, it's more than that. As an airline hostess…

TULIP

Flight attendant.

MABEL

Whatever. Okay, as a LIAT flight attendant you get a lot of practice dealing with people...

TULIP

Tell me about it.

MABEL

But it's more than that.

JUSTIN

I need a break.

TULIP

Don't we all?

MABEL

I have drinks and snacks in my car. Let's go.

TULIP

No. The boys should stay. I don't want Vere to see Kyle just yet.

MABEL

Good call.

(Tulip and Mabel exit)

JUSTIN

Ready to give up university for about a year? Maybe two?

KYLE

If the cause is good, sure.

JUSTIN

Well, ah got a call today assuring me it's 99.9% certain we getting the contract.

KYLE

Which one?

JUSTIN

Which one? Only one of them matter, me boy, the new National Cultural Centre.

KYLE

And the point one percent?

JUSTIN

Funding. Funding is the only hold up now.

KYLE

The one thing that matters.

JUSTIN

Kyle, why you always have to be such a damn ole man?

KYLE

What you talking bout?

JUSTIN

Get excited about something, nuh man. Just this once, take it on faith we will find the money. And when we do, I'm going to hire you full time.

KYLE

I'm flattered, man, but I'm not ready for anything nearly that big.

JUSTIN

Ah know that. That's why I'm hiring the best structural engineer in the region and teaming you up with him. Your job would be to act like a human sponge soaking up everything.

KYLE

That I can surely do, trust me.

(Tulip enters)

TULIP

Kyle, go take a leak, run-around the building...

KYLE

And run in to Mr. Man?

TULIP

No. Not that. Do some push ups in the back, whatever. I need a few minutes alone with your boss.

KYLE

You got it.

(Kyle leaves. Tulip approaches Justin)

TULIP

Every day I get more and more fed up with you.

JUSTIN

Look, I'm sorry, okay? I'm sorry.

TULIP

If you insist on talking to me like I'm some ole dog, you will wake up one day and not have me to talk to.

41

JUSTIN
Well, I don't want that to happen.

TULIP
What's going on with you, Justin?

JUSTIN
What you mean what's going on with me? Everything good. In fact, never better. I was just telling Kyle it look like we getting the contract to build the new Cultural Centre. The only hold up now is funding. We just need to source the money.

TULIP
You drinking again.

JUSTIN
Drinking? What the hell drinking?

TULIP
I know you drinking. And I know you don't want to hear this, but it's way past time for you to get help.

JUSTIN
You right, I don't want to hear it.

(Pause)

Look Tulip, let me explain. Other than you, my daughter, and my day wok, designing and building costumes is my whole life. You know that.

TULIP
Yes.

JUSTIN
But is not enough to design and build, costumes have to be presented properly.

JUSTIN (Continued)

None of my costumes ever been presented properly. I'd like to see that happen at least once before I go to my grave. I want to work with a disciplined group eager to go places none of us ever went before. I call meetings but nobody come. Tonight when you came late I lost it.

(Mabel returns, but seeing Justin and Tulip in deep dialog, holds back. She is joined later by Kyle, then Sauna and she holds them back too)

TULIP

I only came late because the gift I ordered was late. But you're sidestepping the real issue here.

JUSTIN

What gift?

TULIP

For our daughter's wedding.

JUSTIN

For my daughter's wedding?

TULIP

Well, if that's how you insist on seeing it.

JUSTIN

I insist. You want daughter? Give me the child I asking you for so long.

(Long pause)

TULIP

Listen, Justin, I will never have a child for you as long...

43

JUSTIN
Say it! Go ahead and spell it out!

TULIP
Look, I was late because I just don't want to show up at your daughter's wedding with my two long empty hands. The gift wasn't quite ready so I waited because I don't have the time to go back for it before we leave. That's all.

JUSTIN
You think I'm a drunk. That's what you 'fraid to frigging tell me.

TULIP
Justin! Look…the others are back, so back off. Come on guys I see you. Stop spying. Let's get this show on the road.

(The others come forward)

JUSTIN
But you not going to the wedding.

TULIP
Justin…

JUSTIN
You not frigging going to my daughter's goddam wedding.

TULIP
Okay, I'm not going.

JUSTIN
(Addressing the group)

44

JUSTIN

Tulip want to come with me to my daughter's wedding in Miami this weekend.

MABEL

So?

JUSTIN

If she come, who goin' be here to feed my dog?

(He laughs long and hard. The others remain silent)

MABEL

You didn't just say that.

JUSTIN

A joke, people. A stupid little joke.

MABEL

You stupid man, apologize to Tulip right away.

JUSTIN

Wha' wrong with you people?

MABEL

You hear me?

JUSTIN

Nobody could make a little joke anymore?

MABEL

Apologize to Tulip or I done.

JUSTIN

Come on! I will apologize, but what's wrong with us? We cyan laugh an' joke wid each other no more?

45

MABEL

What is joke for crapaud is death for cockroach.

JUSTIN

Listen, Tulip, I didn't mean anything...

TULIP

I don't want your apology.

(Addressing the others)

Ley him take his damn apology and stick it where the
sun doan shine.

JUSTIN

(Acknowledging Sauna)

Look who's back. Hey, little girly, how you manage...

(Sauna walks away from Justin)

She made it back, the little hot mouth...

TULIP

Continue, Mabel.

MABEL

You sure?

TULIP

I'm sure.

MABEL

Okay...you ready, Sauna?

SAUNA

Ready.

MABEL

Kyle?

KYLE

Ready.

MABEL

Justin?

JUSTIN

Sure.

MABEL

Let's get on with it then. The only people who refused to believe the yellow fever story were the slaves. They discussed it among themselves and agreed Uncle was killed by his nephew's beautiful wife for his money. Sarah now had two major problems. The first was how to dispose of all the money in Uncle's strong oak box? Where could she hide it for later use? She soon came up with a plan but needed help.

(Lights come up on Tulip in the past as Sarah)

SARAH

Sofie! Sofia! Where is that lazy girl? Sofia, you don't hear me calling you?

(Sauna comes to Sarah as Sofie)

SOFIE

Here I is, mam.

SARAH

What kept you?

SOFIE

I was hanging out de clothes I wash for you.

47

SARAH

When I call you, you must drop whatever you are doing and come running.

SOFIE

Yes, mam, it will never happen again, mam.

SARAH

Have you finished the small crocus bags I asked you to sew for me?

SOFIE

Just a few left to finish, mam.

SARAH

What's taking you so long?

SOFIE

Is plenty, mam.

SARAH

See to it you bring me every last one of them tomorrow. No excuse. Then every day after, I want you to come to me before sunrise, but after the master leaves. You understand?

SOFIE

Yes, mam.

SARAH

This is a very important job for which I will give you three of my old frocks to wear to church. But you must tell no one about it. It must be a secret between just the two of us. You understand?

SOFIE

Yes, mam.

SARAH

Run along now. Do a good job and I'll throw in some of my bloomers and stockings as well.

(Lights change from past to present)

MABEL

That was how she moved the money. But the crocus bags though small were heavy, so by the third day, Sofie got Sarah's permission to bring Clem, a slave she knew loved her, to help. They had to move the money to an uninhabited lodge about 300 yards away from the main house. Sarah supervised the burying of the money in the cellar and various places around the lodge. On the second to last day of transporting the bags, Clem spoke to Sofie.

CLEM

We almost done move an' bury de money now.

SOFIE

Wha' money?

CLEM

Doan play stupid.

SOFIE

I doan know wha' you talking about.

CLEM

Sofie, is dead me an' you dead. You no see that?

SOFIE

De misses will never kill me.

CLEM

The two of us.

49

SOFIE

You maybe but not me.

CLEM

Ghel, ah neva know you so stupid. You know wha we carrying in dese bags here?

SOFIE

No, an ah doan want to know either.

CLEM

Doan want to know will kill you quicker than poison. Play stupid but doan ever be stupid.

SOFIE

Ah doan know what stupidness you come telling me this morning.

CLEM

Sofia, we hiding de money Master Tom bring wid him from Ireland. De money he get kill for. When we done you think she goin bet to kill us? We have to run way.

SOFIE

Shut you mouth, boy. Ah look stupid enough to go run way wid you?

CLEM

Wha' wrong with me?

SOFIE

What wrong with you?

CLEM

You doan understand' is life an' death ah talking 'bout?

SOFIE

Boy, just hurry up les get the misses work done.

CLEM

Running way is the onliest ting could save us now.

SOFIE

Stop you stupidness an' I might put in a good word wid misses for you. Make her turn you into a good house nigger. Hurry!

(They hurry off. Lights out on past, up on Mabel who speaks directly to the audience)

MABEL

After they finish hiding the treasure, Sarah had to deal with her second problem. How to account for all of Uncle Tom's money disappearing. Immediately after his death she replaced the lock on his bedroom door with a special lock that she had the only key for. She told everybody Uncle's ghost was always in his room sitting on his oak chest. As you can imagine, no one wanted to go near there after dark. Also, she claimed uncle instructed her on his deathbed not to let anyone near his money for ten days, until he came back on the '9 Night' to give instructions about what to do with it. When Patrick dared to question her about this, she flew into a rage.

(Lights fade on present and come up on Sarah walking toward Patrick)

SARAH

You called.

PATRICK

I wish to arrange for the reading of Uncle Tom's will.

51

SARAH

Did you open it?

PATRICK

No. He requested that you and everyone else on the plantation be present.

SARAH

Good. Nothing must be done until after the 9 Night. Understand me clearly, Patrick, nothing.

(She walks away and he follows)

PATRICK

Really, Sarah, what is it with you and this 9 Night?

SARAH

Are you calling me a liar, Patrick?

PATRICK

No, I'm not. I'm simply saying that Uncle took it as a badge of honor that he had no superstitions. I find it hard to believe...

SARAH

You are calling me a liar!

PATRICK

You will hear me out! How could a man who all his life refused to believe in such things ask you to hold a 9...

SARAH

I will not stand for this! I will return to England alone rather than live with a man who calls me a liar to my face! A liar! How could you do this to me, Patrick?

PATRICK

Alright, we are not far from the 9ᵗʰ night of Uncle's death. Let us see how it goes. Let's see if his spirit does indeed return and talks to us. So hold your 9 Night, to which I shall bring Uncle Tom's will. Hopefully, after that we can get on with our lives.

KYLE

Hold up a bit. What's a 9 Night?

MABEL

I forgot you young people don't know anything about culture and history. It's said that nine nights after a person dies, his or her spirit comes back to say goodbye to loved ones. So those loved ones hold a ritual with food, lots of rum and music. Drumming especially. Sometime during the night the spirit will possess one of the dancers causing that dancer to turn. That is, turn into the dead person.

KYLE

Oooh. Never heard of it.

MABEL

So, now you know. Okay, through Sofie, Sarah arranged the 9 Night ritual. Sofie was to be the main dancer with Clem supporting her. On that night Clem was nowhere to be found, but nothing was going to stop Sarah's show. Everybody gathered and soon the drumming started up. Sofie danced, and danced, and danced till she collapsed. But not before she called on her mother to help her.

(While Mabel speaks, the drums and dance begin, softly, slowly)

MABEL (Continued)

(When she is finished music and dance build to a frenzy until Sofie is possessed by Uncle Tom's spirit. She collapses on the ground, then slowly stands upright and speaks slowly and clearly in Uncle's voice)

SOFIE

I have come for my money. I need my money, so I have come for it.

(Sofie spins and stumbles around the stage drunkenly until she collapses again on the floor in a sitting position. Head bent low. The drums beat softly)

PATRICK

What does that mean? I have come for my money?

SARAH

I don't know. Go quick, check uncle's room and see.

(He runs off quickly and shouts from off)

PATRICK

God almighty!

SARAH

What happened?

(Patrick walks back on, stricken)

PATRICK

The box is completely empty. Not a crown left in it.

SARAH

Oh my God! Uncle came for his money.

PATRICK

Let's see what Uncle had to say when he was alive.

(Patrick pulls Uncle's will out of his pocket)

SARAH

God have mercy on us.

PATRICK

Here is the last Will and Testament of one Thomas Flynn.

(He opens and reads it)

It has just one line.

SARAH

For God's sake, what are you waiting for? Read it!

PATRICK

All of my treasures and worldly possessions I leave to my nephew Patrick Rumsey to carry out my wish to have all of the children of Antigua educated.

SARAH

No wonder then that he changed his mind and came back for his money.

(Sofie falls back on the floor, out of it)

PATRICK

What's wrong with her? Sofie! Sofie get up.

(He goes to her and takes her pulse)

She's dead.

SARAH

Lord have mercy on us all.

LIGHTS FADE TO BLACK.

Act II

(The setting is the same as Act I. In the dark we hear the door open and footsteps entering the building. Justin shouts)

JUSTIN

Hellooooooo! Anybody here? Anybody home?

(He turns on the lights)

Nobody! Goddamn nobodies every frigging last one o' them. Nobodies!

(Assuming a Shakespearean manner)

To be a nobody or not to be, that is the question... Sirs, I am sixty years old. I have lived all my life like a wild beast in hiding — a nobody. People forget me, like the mist on Monkey Mountain... How about this: Crowd o' people... crowd of nobodies, gather at my feet let me piss on you! That is the only way you will get enlightenment. Not from your schools and sure as hell not from your goddam churches!—with their high priests in frocks and masquerade hats straddling... no... make that stunting... the earth. You mendicants have allowed both to turn your brains so far off you can never turn them on again in a 100 light years. But I will piss on you and make you whole again... I will...

(Tulip and Mabel enter)

TULIP

Justin, you in here talking to yourself?

MABEL

He playing he is Shakespeare, man.

JUSTIN

Two more late as always mendicants…

TULIP

Justin! Stop it. First of all, we are not late.

JUSTIN

You are late!

TULIP

We are at least 40 minutes early.

(Checking the time)

35 minutes to be exact.

JUSTIN

Did I mess up the time?

TULIP

Just as you messing up your whole life.

JUSTIN

You're an asshole, Tulip, a real asshole.

(To Mabel)

You too.

(Offering his hand to Mabel)

Good night, asshole.

(Mabel whips off a shoe and holds it up, poised to bash in his head)

57

MABEL

Come touch me, nuh. Come ahead man. Just so much as lay that hand on me ley me show you how real life go.

JUSTIN

(Backing off)

Hey, no disrespect.

MABEL

No disrespect? You disrespect Tulip everyday. You disrespect yourself everyday. But it's not okay for you to disrespect me.

(He bends his head and walks away drained)

TULIP

Justin.

(Turning him gently towards her)

What happen? What happen today?

JUSTIN

Lost the contract.

TULIP

For the new cultural centre?

(He nods his head but remains silent)

How come? You didn't win the bid?

JUSTIN

We did, but they didn't have the money, till China came calling.

TULIP

And, don't tell me, their condition is they must build it using their people and materials.

JUSTIN

You got it.

TULIP

No free money. So with the British, so with the Americans, so with the Chinese.

MABEL

Nothing for nothing.

TULIP

Beggars could never be choosers.

(Tulip exits backstage of the old theatre)

MABEL

Justin, I'm sorry to hear. I know you would build a great cultural centre.

JUSTIN

Is not just the building you know, Mabel, is what we could do with it. The programs, the shows we could mount. Goddam dis frigging shit hole of a place to hell!

TULIP

Justin man, one door close we open another.

JUSTIN

With what money?

TULIP

(Tulip comes back on with a pillow)

Yeah, money.

(Pause)

Come, lay down. Take a little rest till we start.

JUSTIN

Wha' rest you telling me 'bout, woman?

TULIP

Come man, it will do you good.

(She makes him comfortable on the ground)

Close your eyes. That's it. Now force your body to relax. Count sheep.

(To Mabel)

Look at that. Fast asleep a'ready.

MABEL

You enable him.

TULIP

I know.

MABEL

You have to stop it.

TULIP

I know that too.

MABEL

I'm serious, Tulip. It's good that you want to help him, but I don't think what we're trying here is going to work. Particularly now with this new blow.

TULIP

You don't think the play is a good idea?

MABEL

I think it's a great idea and support it 100 percent. But I don't think it's going to accomplish what you want.

TULIP

When his mind is occupied, he doesn't drink.

MABEL

Tulip.

TULIP

Well, not as much.

MABEL

Stop deluding yourself. My husband was an alcoholic too. Just like you, I made excuses for him for years, until the day he missed the key of his brain and slap me across my face. Twice. Twice. That very day, I waited until he left the house, picked up my two eight year old pickney dem and made it back to my parent's house in Willikies. Six years later he was dead.

TULIP

And that's exactly what I don't want to see happen to Justin.

61

MABEL

Unfortunately, one daughter inherited that degenerate gene.

TULIP

Don't go there Mabel.

MABEL

Why it had to be her driving home from the graduation party?

TULIP

Stop it, Mabel.

MABEL

All four in the car gone. My two daughters taken away from me by one blow.

TULIP

Mabel, don't go over it again now, please.

MABEL

No, no. I'm done. Like everything else, pain dies. Or at least dulls. But, I want grandchildren even more than I wanted children.

(Sauna and Kyle enter)

SAUNA

Yoo-hoo, we're here.

KYLE

Nite folks.

TULIP

Hey!

MABEL

It's about time.

SAUNA

Five minutes late but ready to get stated. Where's Mr. Excellence?

(Mabel points him out with a movement of her head)

KYLE

What's wrong with him?

TULIP

Tired.

SAUNA

How was the wedding, Auntie?

TULIP

The wedding was fine. Bride looked beautiful, but...

KYLE

(Moving towards Justin)

Hey, Justin, you...

TULIP

No, don't get him up yet.

MABEL

Alright, let's get to it.

TULIP

One minute, Mabel.

TULIP (Continued)

(To Sauna and Kyle)

How the two of you?

SAUNA

We're here, aren't we?

TULIP

And your dad?

SAUNA

Coming around. Mother helping me with him.

TULIP

Now, that's good.

SAUNA

I don't think he's comfortable yet with the new me, though.

TULIP

He'll get accustom.

MABEL

Wait now, I never heard what happened.

SAUNA

Well, that night when I went out to him, we quarreled until he said he's taking me home right away. I said, and what happen to my things? He said go get them and don't let me have to come get you.

MABEL

You joking.

SAUNA

That's when I lost it. I said, "Daddy, beginning now, you need to understand that I'm a woman. I'm no longer a child. As a matter of fact, I am not coming home with you. And if you dare to come in there for me, the next time you see me would be when I come for my things. I got out and slammed the door. I'm surprised he didn't come after me.

MABEL

Good for you, girl, good for you.

SAUNA

Tonight when Kyle came for me he started to make a fuss and Mother said: Sauna, make this is the last time you leave this house and me and your father don't know who you going with. And get this, bring the young man for lunch Sunday so we could meet him. Kyle?

KYLE

You too chupid.

(They both laugh)

TULIP

An' wha' Vere say?

SAUNA

Didn't wait to hear, Auntie. I was through the door.

(They all laugh)

MABEL

You bad girl you. Ready for the big meet up Kyle?

KYLE

Been ready.

MABEL

That's mah boy. I'm so glad for the two of you.

SAUNA

One sec, please. Auntie, you said the bride was beautiful but…What's the but?

TULIP

Can't really get into that now.

SAUNA

Tell me, Auntie, please.

TULIP

Very briefly. I'm in a predicament and need all of you to help me.

SAUNA

What happen?

TULIP

Justin made a total fool of himself.

MABEL

As was to be expected.

TULIP

He started out in such great spirits. She looked marvelous and he walked her down the aisle, all smiles. Back to being his charming ole self. The ceremony, the decor, the food, everything was perfect as he paid for it to be.

TULIP (Continued)

Then when he was giving his toast he looked across at his ex, sitting there with her third new husband and went off.

MABEL

You lie!

TULIP

Completely lost it, Mabel, and it wasn't pretty.

SAUNA

What happened?

TULIP

Nooo. Not now. All I would say is Justin needs help and as his friends we must help him.

KYLE

He has mine, 100 percent.

SAUNA

Eh, eh, you well quick.

TULIP

I need help with him.

SAUNA

Of course, Auntie, You have my support. Justin too.

MABEL

Everybody done know where I stand.

67

TULIP

Thanks.

(She hugs each of them individually)

Thank you all so much.

(Pause)

Now, let's get on with the story.

MABEL

Where were we again?

SAUNA

Sarah had just poisoned her husband's uncle for his money and got away with it by plotting and scheming. Or did she?

MABEL

Well, that's what we're going to find out. She did manage to get all of the money hidden away. She did manage to get away with two murders, Uncle Tom and Sofia. So, on the one hand you could say Sarah got away with it, or, as Sauna just asked, did she?

SAUNA

Well?

MABEL

One thing Sarah didn't bargain for was the response of the slaves. They loved Uncle Tom because he never treated them less than human. Word about his and Kinta's education plan had spread around the island faster than by Internet, so they felt a deep sense of loss and took action.

KYLE

Like what?

MABEL

Sarah got to see passive aggressive centuries before history gave it a name. Everything she tried was sabotaged. And her frustration was heightened by the second problem she had not foreseen.

SAUNA

Hope it drove her crazy.

MABEL

Worse than that. Patrick became so saddened by his Uncle's death he was often too drunk to be of use to her, himself, or anyone else. Their once thriving plantation started going downhill fast. She paced the house nightly, plotting her exit.

(Lights cross fade to Sarah in the house, pacing)

SARAH

Patrick! Patrick, get in here now.

(Justin joins her as Patrick)

PATRICK

Why are you making such a terrible din, dear?

SARAH

I beg your pardon?

PATRICK

Why the racket? Why are you hollering at me like that?

SARAH

How dare you talk to me in such a manner?

PATRICK

What did my uncle do to deserve to die?

SARAH

You are drunk!

PATRICK

What did he do?

SARAH

Rum gives you the courage to bring this crazy talk to me at every turn? Drunken reprobate! Why don't you bring it to me when you're sober? Coward! You are a groveling, mincing, sniveling coward! Who didn't even have the smarts to get enough from your rich uncle for a decent life.

PATRICK

We have enough!

SARAH

Enough so that we could at least visit frequently if not live in the civilized, intellectual capitals of the world.

PATRICK

What's wrong with living here?

SARAH

Everything is wrong with living here. From the burning heat to the ugly, stupid, bumbling slaves.

PATRICK

My uncle did leave me wealthy, and by extension my wife. You could have been the legitimate owner of his fortune.

SARAH

He was going to blow his money on the crazy notion of teaching black slaves to read and write.

PATRICK

He wanted you to work on the project with…

SARAH

Shut up! I don't want to hear it.

PATRICK

Why did you not tell me the British sold your parents as slaves for bad debt?

SARAH

Who told you that?

PATRICK

Uncle did.

SARAH

He is a liar! That is a damn lie! Your uncle was a stupid fool and a stinking, dirty liar. I'm sick of him, I'm sick of you, I'm sick of this God forsaken place. God!

(Long pause)

It is just as well you hear it now. I'm leaving you.

PATRICK

You are?

SARAH

The next ship that leaves for England will leave with me on it.

PATRICK

Good.

SARAH

Now, if you don't mind, I must locate the luggage your uncle brought so I can begin packing my things.

(Crossfade to the present)

MABEL

With that, Sarah began to prepare for her departure. That evening she entered Uncle Tom's bedroom with her gas lantern. Soon after, there were numerous claps of thunder in the distance. This sent Patrick to look for her.

(Patrick approaches her in the 'bedroom')

PATRICK

There is a storm brewing.

SARAH

I do not want to be disturbed.

PATRICK

Sounds like it will be fierce.

SARAH

Leave me alone.

PATRICK

Please, Sarah, this is no time to be alone.

SARAH

Start practicing.

PATRICK

I'm not talking about me I'm…

SARAH

I'm comfortable being alone. Stay away from me.

(She slams the 'door' in his face and he walks away. Patrick sits up stage, back to the audience)

MABEL

Now remember, after Uncle's death, she had put a lock on the door for which she had the only key.

(There is a mighty clap of thunder)

The thunder startled her, causing her to trip and fall. Now that would not normally be a huge problem, but the lantern she was carrying broke, spilling oil all over her nightdress. Soon she and the room were ablaze.

SARAH

Patrick! Patrick, help me! Please Patrick help me!

(Patrick rushes to the room and tries to open the door without luck. He throws his shoulder against it but it doesn't budge)

PATRICK

Unlock the door.

SARAH

I can't get up.

PATRICK

Crawl and push the key under.

SARAH

Break it down.

MABEL

Slaves arrived with pit-axes and a crowbar. They broke down the door and Patrick rushed in to save his wife.

(Patrick brings Sarah on stage in his arms, cradles her body and weeps. Lights slowly fade to black. A long music bridge. Lights come up on the present with all five actors together)

MABEL

Patrick did his very best, but Sarah Rumsey was no more.

SAUNA

Good. She got what she deserved.

MABEL

But the story doesn't end there. Soon after her death, her ghost was seen at the lodge that is no longer there, at her house that still is, on the road in between, and in the area generally.

SAUNA

I doan want to hear 'bout no ghost.

KYLE

I goin' protect you, man, doan worry. Go on, Mabel.

MABEL

Well, according to legend, from Sarah Rumsey's death to now, over three hundred and fifty years later, her ghost has put in a regular appearance.

SAUNA

And people see it?

MABEL

Sometimes even in the broad daylight, they say.

KYLE

Who say?

MABEL

Numerous eyewitness reports over the centuries.

KYLE

I say, nutn tall go so.

MABEL

Say wha' you want.

KYLE

Soon come.

(He exits)

MABEL

Sometimes in the moonlight the ghost is seen in the form of a beautiful woman, with a lighted lamp in the left hand. On the lamp, the numbers 8.9.1.6 are usually displayed, but not always in the same order. Anyway, by far the most remarkable report is from a man called Jack Collins who in 1866 was determined to meet face to face with this ghost.

JACK/KYLE

I did try vigorously to meet with this fabled ghost. But after several failed attempts I gave up, dismissing the ghost stories as idle gossip. Then, about six months after, I was driving home one night and saw a brilliant light rapidly approaching me. When I noticed that the light was not on the road but was coming toward me as if carried by some person floating in mid-air, I whipped up my horse trying to escape the encounter. But the light came nearer and nearer until at last the figure was standing motionless directly ahead of me. My horse slackened its pace and came to a halt, snorting and trembling a few yards from the figure. I fell upon the ground trembling.

SAUNA

Jesus, god! Stop! Ah cyan take it!

TULIP

Doan let no stupid ghost story frighten you, girl.

JACK

I mustered up enough courage to look up, and were I to live a thousand years I could never describe the loveliness of the woman I saw walking slowly toward me, holding a lighted lamp which became less and less brilliant, until it was totally extinguished when she reached my side. Then there was a hail of brilliant rays emitting from her lantern the numbers 6.8.9.1. I have never been more terrified as when I found myself in total darkness with the ghost. I tried to speak. I urged my horse forward, but I could do neither, so I sat there petrified. The 'thing' said distinctly ...

JACK (Continued)

(Heard over speakers)

"SEEK HER AT LA RUE DE LA PAIX IN PARIS, AND SHE WILL TELL YOU ALL".

JACK

But as I had never been to Paris and knew no one there, I did not go.

MABEL

However, some sixteen years later, when he had almost forgotten about the incident, he found himself in Paris where he watched a stagecoach overturn. Most of the passengers were merely shaken, but a young lady lay motionless in the street, apparently unconscious.

(Jack rushes to the young woman lying on the street and picks her up and carries her)

YOUNG WOMAN

Thank you. I can walk from here.

(She makes a few steps but stumbles)

Help me to the Hotel Normandy where my father and I are staying.

(Jack walks around the stage in a semi-circle with her leaning on him)

I can manage from here, thank you for your help.

(She exits quickly)

YOUNG WOMAN (Contd)

(Off)

Oh, Father, it is he. We met today in La Rue de la Paix.

JACK

La Rue de la Paix? Goodness gracious me!

(Addressing the audience)

It is only now I recognize the connection between the phantom of the Parham Road in Antigua 16 years ago and now. "Seek her in la Rue de la Paix in Paris and she will tell you all". I must go directly to her tomorrow.

(Jack moves into position and waits. After two beats, the Young Woman appears with her hand extended. Jack takes it gently)

JACK

I hope you have fully recovered from yesterday's accident.

YOUNG WOMAN

I have, thanks to you.

(She motions him to a chair)

YOUNG WOMAN

I know this must all seem very strange to you. Unfortunately, it must get even stranger yet.

JACK

Well, I certainly would like to…

YOUNG WOMAN

No. Don't speak, listen.

(Pause)

Centuries ago, one of my ancestors sold her soul to demons for the lust of gold. Because of the horrible deed she committed, Heaven decreed her to a sentence of wandering day and night, wretched and restless, as punishment.

JACK

But surely...

YOUNG WOMAN

Please. This phantom shall continue to wander in misery and atone for her sins until such time that two maidens pure, come as brides simultaneously and occupy the houses at both ends of the haunted road in Parham. This shall lift the curse from her family and especially from me.

JACK

From you? Why you?

YOUNG WOMAN

It is too painful. Which is why you must help me.

JACK

Well, I will...I will do my best, but...

YOUNG WOMAN

When you return to Antigua, seek once more the phantom, and tell her that her time of purgatory now numbers only fourteen years.

JACK

How do you know?

YOUNG WOMAN

In my sleep last night, I saw a silver-winged, flying chariot guided by a quiver-laden lad somewhat like cupid.

JACK

What does that mean?

YOUNG WOMAN

The mystic numbers 1-8-9-6 were inscribed on the panels of this flying chariot. In it were two brides arranged in all the splendor of their tropic wedding dresses and it was traveling toward the haunted road. The numbers were finally in the correct order, 1-8-9-6, 1896. That is the year when my ancestor and I can finally know peace.

JACK

Am I to understand then, that you want me to...

YOUNG WOMAN

Yes, I want you to meet with the phantom soon, to alert her that the end of her penance draws nigh. Then I want you to meet her again in 1896, 14 years from now, that she may tell you where the treasure is hidden. Good bye.

JACK

Hold up. I need to know...

YOUNG WOMAN

I am telling you, listen well. Thirty minutes before the expiration of these fourteen years, the Parham Ghost, then on its last pilgrimage, will disclose the spot where the treasure is hidden. I urge you to be there to claim it.

JACK

Please. Tell me…

YOUNG WOMAN

I have told you everything you need to know. Make contact with my relative when you get back to Antigua. Then meet with her again in 1896 when she will tell you where to find the treasure. I want you to have this great fortune. I want this to be my gift to you for helping me.

(She puts out her hand)

Thank you for your interest and patience. We leave Paris this midnight, farewell.

(Crossfade to Mabel in the present)

MABEL

In February 1883 he arrived back in Antigua. But for some unknown reason disregarded the instructions to renew his acquaintance with the Ghost. He even avoided mentioning the subject or passing near that haunted road. It seemed he didn't want to encounter the ghost again even to learn where that fabulous treasure is hidden.

TULIP

Smart man.

JUSTIN

Smart man? That's a very foolish man.

TULIP

You would say that.

JUSTIN

Wha' you mean by that?

TULIP

Just go ahead, Mabel.

SAUNA

Hold up, wha' happen to all the money?

MABEL

Still out there waiting for somebody to claim.

KYLE

So nothing happened in 1896?

MABEL

Nothing. And remember, this was the last chance the ghost had to tell where she hid the gold. And if she didn't her soul would be forever damned. Now on the appointed night, the two brides where there, one in each house, and people say that 30 minutes to midnight there was the most brilliant light at the crossroads. But neither Jack Collins, nor anyone else, was there to meet the ghost and claim the gold.

SAUNA

So all that good gold just out there? Somewhere?

KYLE

Question is where?

MABEL

Wait. There's more.

SAUNA

More?

MABEL

Yeah.

JUSTIN

Tell us, Mabel.

MABEL

Over a year ago, Ma Hennie on her deathbed had a dream with a new revelation. The ghost is longing for her soul to be at piece and managed to get a reprieve.

JUSTIN

What you saying?

MABEL

On any given full moon now, anyone can meet the ghost in the crossroads at Parham and she will tell them where to find the treasure.

SAUNA

For real?

MABEL

But there're conditions.

TULIP

Always conditions.

JUSTIN

Let's hear them.

MABEL

The person must be in the right spot, directly under the moon, exactly 30 minutes before midnight on a clear night. And it can't be any ole riff-raff either. It must be a person of good character for the ghost to even show. And he or she must use 90% of the money for some cause that will benefit the whole island, such as what Uncle Tom Flynn wanted to do.

JUSTIN

But Mabel, how come ah never heard that part of the story before?

MABEL

Most people. And I would say it's the most important part today.

JUSTIN

You think?

TULIP

Justin, let's leave this alone.

JUSTIN

Nar, man, I think we may have a golden opportunity here.

SAUNA

Me too, for sure.

JUSTIN

Look, Sarah Rumsey was a real person. She and her husband did run a plantation here in Parham. And she did murder Uncle Thomas Flynn and hid his gold, right?

MABEL

According to both legend and history. Yes!

KYLE

And guess what, tonight is a great night to go looking for this lost treasure.

SAUNA

Meaning?

KYLE

Tonight we have the right conditions for the ghost to appear.

SAUNA

Whaaaaat!

MABEL

For true?

KYLE

Absolutely. Full moon, clear night, the crossroads within walking distance, the...

JUSTIN

Stop. I think we should go.

TULIP
Go where?

JUSTIN
I think we should give it a shot.

TULIP
Give what a shot?

JUSTIN
We should try to meet with the ghost.

MABEL
Ah ready.

SAUNA
I ready too.

KYLE
Let's go!

TULIP
You all cyan be serious?

JUSTIN
Wha' we have to lose?

TULIP
It's nonsense. 'Nancy story that's all.

JUSTIN
Is fraid you fraid ghost?

TULIP
How I goin' fraid wha' I doan believe in?

SAUNA

Please, Aunty…

TULIP

Listen…

SAUNA

I fraid ghost and I still want to go.

TULIP

I ain't in any foolishness with you all, you know.

MABEL

Humor us.

SAUNA

Aunty, man, doan be a spoil sport. Please. Please, please, please.

TULIP

Okay, Okay, I'll humor you.

JUSTIN

Good! Let's go.

TULIP

(Holding out her hand)

I'll drive.

JUSTIN

I'm driving.

TULIP

No, give me the keys.

87

JUSTIN

You think I'm drunk?

TULIP

I think…I think I drive better than you at night.

JUSTIN

You think I'm an ass?

TULIP

No.

JUSTIN

Wha' de hell wrong with you, woman. Why you always want to embarrass me like this?

TULIP

I'm not trying to em…

JUSTIN

Ah heard you tonight you know. I heard you talking out my business.

TULIP

I wasn't talk…

JUSTIN

You were! You goddamn well was. You told them I made a fool of myself.

TULIP

And you did! Goddamn it, man, you made a fool of yourself. And you promised me…

88

KYLE

Look, I hate to interrupt this, but the one thing against us is time.

TULIP

Forget it. All you go ahead.

MABEL

No, Tulip, we ain't going without you. I'll drive. Besides, of the five of us, you're the one the ghost most likely to talk to.

TULIP

If I go, I'm walking.

MABEL

Let's all walk.

KYLE & SAUNA

Walk!

MABEL

It's just up the road. Five... ten minutes at the most.

JUSTIN

We have time, Kyle?

KYLE

If we hurry, yes.

JUSTIN

Then let's go.

(They exit Down Left, then reappear Up Right and walk across the back of the stage up onto the platform, to the crossroads)

JUSTIN

Okay, Kyle, help me find the exact spot where she has to be.

(Kyle and Justin move around, looking at the moon, pacing out the spot)

KYLE

Here.

JUSTIN

Yeah. That looks right to me. Come, Tulip, stand right here.

(Tulip moves into position)

How much time left?

KYLE

Less than a minute.

TULIP

Good. Let's get this nonsense over and be done with it.

(A bright white light engulfs them all, then narrows to a pencil spot on Tulip. The others kneel)

SAUNA

Jesus have mercy on us.

(Dead silence, followed by a sound that suggests the ghost is about to speak. Tulip becomes engulfed in a struggle with herself that suggests she's fighting for possession. She pulls herself out of the spot and runs down the steps pausing briefly to look back. The spot vanishes and lights return to normal)

MABEL

Tulip!?

(Tulip runs off, retraces her route and ends up where she started in the old school hall. The others soon follow)

JUSTIN

You los' you mind, woman?

SAUNA

What happen, Aunty?

JUSTIN

You los' you frigging mind?

SAUNA

The ghost was ready to speak.

JUSTIN

Couldn't be more ready.

SAUNA

Yes!

JUSTIN

Think of all we coulda do with that money! We could have built the National Cultural Centre to start with. None of us woulda been in need again.

SAUNA

Never again, for sure!

JUSTIN

You got that right.

TULIP
And when you all going to let me speak?

JUSTIN
You messed up, Tulip! We had the chance…

MABEL
Let Tulip speak please.

TULIP
Thank you, Mabel. It would be nice to have that modern, digital National Cultural Centre, wouldn't it?

JUSTIN
Damn right, it would be.

MABEL
I would welcome it.

KYLE
So would I.

SAUNA
Yes! For sure.

MABEL
It would do the island a lot of good.

TULIP
Then let's build it.

JUSTIN
Build it?

TULIP

Yes. On our own, using our own initiative and talent and brains.

JUSTIN

Look, ah used to think like that, but the hard knocks of reality taught me sense.

TULIP

What sense it makes, standing out there in the middle of the night expecting some ghost to point us to some lousy chest of gold at the end of some rainbow?

JUSTIN

We were there. We had a real chance to check out the legend once and for all. What's wrong with that?

TULIP

I for one could never believe in magic money.

JUSTIN

Did you see…

TULIP

I don't care what I saw.

JUSTIN

Real or not, we had the chance of a life…

TULIP

And I deliberately passed on it because there's no free money. Why you think Jack Collins never went for the money? Because he knew every freeness under the sun comes with conditions - spoken or unspoken.

93

TULIP (Continued)

(Pause)

The other reason I passed, Mr. Justin, is to get your attention.

JUSTIN

Well, you have it.

TULIP

Tonight was the last straw. I will no longer allow you to talk to me like you do. I will no longer make excuses for you. I will no longer put up with you.

JUSTIN

I want to…I'm going to do better.

TULIP

You say that all the time, and I'm done listening.

JUSTIN

I mean it. This time, for sure.

TULIP

I'm done with you, Justin. Done! Done!

JUSTIN

Tulip, ple…

TULIP

You understand that? Done.

(Tulip moves away. Mabel and Sauna go to her in support, but she brushes them off and sits by herself)

MABEL

Well, I done here too.

(She moves to collect her purse and Sauna follows)

JUSTIN

Listen, all of you. I did make myself a big fool at the wedding. And I have been nothing but ashamed since.

MABEL

Well, I'm glad you're admitting it, even if it's too late now.

JUSTIN

As Tulip said, I went all out to make the wedding very special and by the time I stood up to make my toast I was in great spirits, pun intended.

(The others laugh)

No, don't laugh.

SAUNA

How you expect us not to laugh and you giving joke?

JUSTIN

True, but I'm saying this to you, not as a joke. Carmen was sitting there with her third husband, grinning. It seemed to me mocking, as I made my toast, and I went off. I crossed into some other zone where I had no control over body or mind, given over completely to rage and crazed ranting. I called her a whoring bitch in every way and in every language I could.

JUSTIN (Continued)

Things came out of my mouth that I don't want to ever pass my lips again. It was a relief when her brothers punched me to the floor and kicked me almost senseless. As the rage subsided a wave of shame hit me and I laid there begging the earth to open and swallow me.

(He moves into position and lays on the ground)

And then, and then...

(Tulip comes to him)

TULIP

It's going to be alright, Justin, just breath. Breathe deeply and slowly. They have sent for the police. But you're not going down like this. I will not let you go down like this. You hear me? Pull all of your strength together and get up. I will help you. Get up!

(She helps him slowly to his feet and puts her arm around his waist)

Steady now. I got you. Put your arm around my shoulder and let's walk out of here. Hold up your head.

(He does and they walk out of the 'room' to applause)

SAUNA

Auntie Tulip is really something else you know.

MABEL

I know. I woulda leave his sorry ass right there.

KYLE

Then is a good thing is Tulip he has to deal with and not you.

MABEL

Or any other woman.

JUSTIN

The morning after, Cherise came to see me. She told me I did not deserve you and that if I couldn't get my life together I should let you go before I drag you down with me.

TULIP

Your daughter told you that?

JUSTIN

You mean our daughter.

TULIP

Yes, our daughter.

JUSTIN

I promised her faithfully that I would get myself together because I never want to lose you.

TULIP

Too late for that now.

JUSTIN

Don't say that, Tulip, please.

TULIP

I can't go on like this, Justin. You make promises you don't keep. You say you're going to stop drinking...

JUSTIN

I know, I know. I told myself...I kept telling myself...I have the will power to stop whenever I want to. I know better than that now.

TULIP

Do you?

JUSTIN

Yes. Yes, I do.

TULIP

Well, I don't believe you.

JUSTIN

Then try this. I'm going to enroll in Alcoholics Anonymous tomorrow and I promise you I will give it my all. Give me a year and if I'm not doing better don't waste any more time with me, walk away.

TULIP

I don't know about this. I really don't know.

JUSTIN

Sauna, help me...please.

SAUNA

Come on, Auntie Tulip, man, have a heart.

MABEL

She's right, Tulip, you know that.

98

KYLE

So what you say, Auntie Tulip?

JUSTIN

I say, I will need the full support of all of you.

TULIP

And so would I.

MABEL

That you have.

SAUNA

We will all help you.

KYLE

One hundred percent.

TULIP

Then in that case I say, let's give it a shot.

(Justin and Tulip hug and kiss as the others cheer)

KYLE

(Singing loudly)

Hip, hip, hurray!

SAUNA

Hip, hip, hurray!

KYLE

For he's a jolly good fellow...

SAUNA

And she's a very fine lady...

MABEL

(They freeze and Mabel moves away from the group to addresses the audience)

And so it was that on that fateful night Justin pledged to address his problem and has been sober since. He and Tulip are married now for five years. They have a beautiful, smart three your old they christened Mabel and I'm her grandmother. That makes me prouder and happier than you could ever imagine. Sauna joined Kyle at university. Both have since graduated and are doing well. There's talk of marriage in the air, with the full blessing of Sauna's dad.

KYLE & SAUNA

They'll make a jolly good couple...

(They freeze again)

MABEL

As for the treasure, it still has not yet been claimed. Sarah's ghost is seen from time to time, still looking for some decent person to tell where it is hidden. So, if you dare, and of course, if you qualify, do go to the crossroads in Parham on any full-moon night and claim the treasure. That way Sarah Rumsey's soul will finally know peace. Good luck.

KYLE & SAUNA

And so say all of us.

(Mabel moves back to the group and joins the singing which becomes riotous)

ALL

And so say all of us, And so say all of us,
They'll make a jolly good couple,
Which nobody can deny.
Which nobody can deny,
Which nobody can deny.

They'll make a very fine couple (three times)
And so say all of us.

(Light fade to black)

THE END